Stirring Up Memories

Heidi Wigand-Nicely

IngramSpark
1246 Heil Quaker Blvd.
La Vergne, TN 37086
http://www.ingramspark.com

Printed in the United States of America.

First printing, 2021.

ISBN: 9780578952987

What is this book?
It is a treasury of favorite recipes used at Fox Run Bed & Breakfast.
These selected recipes are simple, reliable, have a short prepara-
tion time and use ingredients that are readily available.
Don't want to spend endless hours in the kitchen preparing food?
This is your book.

High Altitude?
Yes, these are suited to high altitude and may need minimal adjustments
and shorter baking/cooking times at altitudes lower than 5000 ft.

Gluten Free?
There are some recipes in this book that are specifically gluten-free, and
others that are by nature as they don't include flour or gluten at all.

Indian Magic Crabapple Tree planted on the property in memory of my dad.

This book is dedicated:

To my great-grandmother, BERGER OMA, who spoke one word of English and made the best kipfel ever.

To KIRCHNER OMA and OPA, who welcomed me with open arms, spoiled me, always worked either in the kitchen, yard or garage (making wine) and who taught me how to ride a bike, which remains a passion of mine today.

To WIGAND OMA, who baked professionally until she was 86 years old.

To my MOM and DAD who set a great example, put up with me and will always live in my heart.

To my BROTHERS, SISTERS-IN-LAW and their FAMILIES, who actually cook a lot more than I do.

To TYLER, HOLLY, ALEX and CODY ... who grew up by the words, "Take it or leave it," and, for the most part, enjoyed everything I made in the kitchen. To this day, none of you even thinks of saying the word "hate" at the table.

To JENNA, MEGAN and LEAH for now putting up with the above-mentioned boys.

With all my love I dedicate this book to the young ones, BRAYDEN, KYLEE, CHARLIE and any future GRANDCHILDREN on the horizon that I haven't yet met. May we have fun creating foods together, and may you remember that even though we make playdough in the kitchen, we do not eat it.

Starters, Sides & Such

Main Breakfast Dishes

Breads & Beyond

Starters, Sides and Such

Oranges with Sour Cream

The brown sugar adds to the tastiness of this dish.

Ingredients (Per serving)

1 unpeeled orange

1 strawberry

⅛ teaspoon brown sugar

1 Tablespoon sour cream

⅛-¼ teaspoon grated orange peel

Sprinkle of cinnamon or nutmeg

Directions

- Slice oranges crosswise (stem to the side) into 4-6 slices. You can keep the ends to flavor water with or use to grate for the "orange zest."

- On each individual slice, cut around inside of peel to remove orange from peel. If you wish to expedite this, you can just peel the orange and then slice, but the edges aren't as "clean" then.

- Place 3-5 slices in small bowl and sprinkle with brown sugar. Let sit for at least 15 minutes or so.

- Top with a spoonful of sour cream or yogurt. Top with grated orange peel, sprinkle with a bit of cinnamon or nutmeg and add strawberry slices to dish.

Fruit Dish Au Gratin

INGREDIENTS (PER SERVING)

2-3 gingersnaps

3-4 heaping Tablespoons of fruit (bite-sized pieces and ramekin should be almost full) These can be raspberries, blueberries, peaches, strawberries or blackberries.

2-3 heaping Tablespoons of yogurt (vanilla or plain)

½ teaspoon honey

¼ teaspoon lemon juice

DIRECTIONS

- Butter bottom and sides of each ramekin dish (small, individual dish).
- Crush gingersnaps with rolling pin and place in bottom of ramekin (crushing them in a Ziploc bag works well).
- Top with chopped fruit.
- Mix yogurt, honey and lemon juice and spoon over fruit.
- Broil on high (about 4" from heat) for approx. 7 minutes - watch closely.
- Remove when first hint of browning and bubbling.

This fruit dish can be eaten before your meal, along with it or for dessert.

The Motor Home

This is a great dish you can make for many people. One of my first bookings was a small family, I thought ... then the motorhome drove up.

At first, I wondered why someone driving a motorhome would need a B&B, but I was of course grateful for the business! They drove around my front circle, turned off the ignition and out came Andrew. After him, out bounced a beautiful, energetic little girl. Next, out stepped her mom. Wait, there's more ... out walked grandpa who came along ... and then grandma who had flown in from another location and was picked up from the airport along the way.

I waited in anticipation ... how many more would emerge from the motor home? Apparently, that was it.

Wonderful, happy group of people, and they had all arrived to watch the little girl compete in track at the United States Air Force Academy which was located about five miles from Fox Run B&B.

She got some great track practice in at my place – the first evening she was so excited to see green grass that she ran directly through the screen door! Dad was very apologetic and fixed it, but to be honest, it really needed replacing and she just helped expedite the process. Memories that bring a smile.

These Fruit Dish au Gratin are delicious. It is best to use a combination of two fruits of different colors. If you have any leftover dishes, refrigerate and eat cold or reheat.

An interesting twist on serving bananas. Most guests had never heard of broiled bananas but were willing to try and really enjoyed them.

These go well with the Southwest Casserole and would be delicious on French toast as well.

Broiled Bananas

INGREDIENTS

¼ cup packed brown sugar

2 Tablespoons jam (I like using apricot, but any flavor can be used)

4 medium-sized, firm bananas

DIRECTIONS

- Peel and slice bananas into approximately ½" slices.
- Lightly grease baking pan (8" x 8" or larger).
- Mix (by hand) brown sugar and jam in small bowl.
- Add banana slices and mix gently to coat bananas with mixture.
- Spread in prepared pan and broil on high for about 5 minutes.
- Bananas should become bubbly and begin to brown. Watch closely.
- Place in small bowls with a spoonful of plain/vanilla yogurt or sour cream on top.
- Serve immediately.

The Schnapps Boot

One thing I never serve for breakfast is schnapps. Here's why I mention it.

I had a German family stay and return for a visit. The woman brought me a gift, a really cute little glass boot about the size of a shot glass. She said it was a Schnapps Boot and was surprised I didn't know that as I am German as well.

She said I could use it for guests. I said, "Diane, I don't think I should be serving guests Schnapps for breakfast."

We resolved it by displaying the boot on the kitchen table, and it does a wonderful job of holding toothpicks.

A yogurt bar goes with any meal really. I normally use vanilla yogurt and add bowls of fruit (fresh or frozen), nuts, craisins, granola ... use your imagination and whatever you have on hand or is in season.

You will make these more than once. A unique way to serve potatoes with your breakfast.

Potatoes in Muffin Tins

Ingredients (Per serving)

1 Red or Gold potato

⅓ cup grated cheddar cheese (or a mix of white/orange cheeses)

1 tomato slice/wedge per cup (or pepper slices if you prefer)

2 Tablespoons Half-and-Half/table cream

Directions

- Thoroughly grease muffin tin (I normally plan on two individual portions per person).
- Slice potatoes into thin round slices. Cover bottom of each portion with a slice.
- Sprinkle grated cheese to cover potato slice.
- Repeat with potato slice and cheese, alternating until tin is full.
- Top each portion with one slice/wedge of tomato or bell pepper.
- Pour two Tablespoons cream over each one.
- Shake salt and pepper over each – also paprika or spice blend of your choice.
- Bake @ 350F 30-45 minutes.
- Start checking after 30 minutes by inserting toothpick – should be soft.
- Remove from oven and loosen each with knife.
- Remove each cup with large spoon and set on platter. Keep warm in oven until ready to serve.

This is a great way to add potatoes to the breakfast, and they are easy to prepare, tasty and great for leftovers. They look really nice on a platter.

Top and season however you choose.

My favorites are tomatoes or sliced sweet peppers: yellow, red and orange of the mini variety.

Seasoning options:
- *Salt & Pepper*
- *Hungarian paprika*
- *Shallots or Chives*
- *Garlic*
- *Tarragon*
- *Basil*
- *Dill*

Kids' Tastes

Kids can invent new food combinations quite creatively. An eight-year-old girl who was staying here with her parents was quite an adventuresome foodie.

When I showed her the strawberry sauce for the crepes, she scanned the buffet, including the yogurt bar, and said, "I think I'll try some of that on my yogurt."

Mm, it was delicious. Why hadn't I thought of that?

I used to put out cold cereal and milk for my guests who had brought children. I thought the young kids would go for that immediately – you know, something familiar and safe. Nope. They looked over the buffet and said, "I'll just try some of this, and this ..." I don't even bother with the cereal anymore.

A brisk winter walk with Jesse after a fresh snowfall at nearby Fox Run Park.

Chocolate Lab

One set of guests consisted of two grandparents and two grandkids, both boys. They had as much fun hanging around the property as they did going out sightseeing. In the afternoon when they had returned from their outings, I would receive a text asking if Jesse, my dog, could come out and play in the backyard. So sweet.

One morning after breakfast I pulled out the tractor to get started on some outside work. As soon as they heard it turn on, they both ran over to check it out.

The older boy looked it over (quite a small tractor in comparison to what I'm sure they were used to), glanced up at me and said, "Let me know if you need anything fixed on it. I'll even cut some grass for you." Hired!

When they returned home to Texas (a sad goodbye), I received a picture of a sweet chocolate lab puppy ... their parents had heard so much about Jesse that they had purchased the puppy as a surprise for the boys upon their return home. Lucky boys, and very lucky dog.

Fried Potatoes

It's nice to have a side of potatoes with your morning breakfast. I use either Red Potatoes or Gold. I slice them into medium-sized chunks and figure about 2 people per potato. I always leave the skin on. Place in frying pan (cast iron is best) with some oil and water (not enough to cover potatoes ... you can always add more if needed). Simmer covered until water is gone and potatoes are almost tender. Add some butter to help with the browning process. You may also want to add any of the items in the paragraph below.

My friend Barb's daughter, Vanessa, who is a chef, said that butter is the secret to browning. Doesn't butter make everything taste better?

My Ute elder friend and President of Native American Sacred Trees and Places (NASTaP), Dr. James Jefferson, always loved having the potatoes when he stayed at the B&B. He liked "all kinds of things" in them including peppers, butter, seasonings, sausage, bacon, onions ... whatever I had on hand. Sometimes we topped them with sour cream as well. What a treat it was to host him.

Hot Chocolate

INGREDIENTS

¼ cup sugar

¼ cup baking cocoa

Dash salt

⅓ cup hot water

4 cups milk

¾ teaspoon vanilla

DIRECTIONS

- Combine sugar, cocoa and salt in pan.
- Add water and boil for 2 minutes while stirring.
- Stir in milk and heat to serving temperature, but do not boil.
- Whisk until frothy.
- Refrigerate leftovers (although you probably won't have any) and heat up in microwave or on stovetop just until warm.

Hot Chocolate Charlie

This recipe always reminds me of Charlie and his family. He and his sister fell in love with my dog, Jesse, and were so sad to leave. I recall them sitting at the top of the stairs with Jesse between them … and there were no dry eyes.

I always show kids where the hot chocolate packets are, and Charlie said, "Oh thanks, but I only drink hot chocolate in the winter." (He's from Texas.)

The next morning, he piped up and exclaimed, "Wow, that hot chocolate tasted so good! It's cold here in the morning!" Yep, even in June.

Of course, the next morning I ran out of hot chocolate packets. Charlie was a bit disappointed.

I said, "Charlie, I am going to make you some REAL hot chocolate." I made it from scratch, using fresh milk, baking cocoa, sugar and vanilla. It was so good that we all had to have a little, and I'm not sure what I had started for Charlie's family … but we convinced him this was special because he was on vacation.

"Don't expect this at home when you return," was the message in his parents' eyes. Come to think of it, I saw that look in lots of guests' eyes.

Properly Pulled Dandelions

An elderly gentleman and his wife came to stay over a weekend to attend their granddaughter's high school graduation. They could not believe we were using the wood burner at night, as it was the end of May. I have a really nice memory of them sitting in the rocking chairs in front of it to enjoy the warmth.

During the day, however, it was blue sky and sunny. In fact, the snow had just melted, and it was the beginning of dandelion season. They seemed to be popping up by the hundreds in my yard.

After breakfast, the guests saw me outside, pulling dandelions and tossing them in a bucket. The tool I was using wasn't particularly efficient.

In truth, if you were a professional landscaper, it would have been downright unacceptable.

In the meantime, the land-line phone would ring occasionally. The guest asked if he should answer it while I was outside and I said no, it was fine to let voicemail handle it and I would call back. About two minutes later he came out and said, "The phone's for you. I thought it might be important, so I answered it." I thanked him and went inside to get it. It was a telemarketer.

The next morning when I went into the kitchen to fix their breakfast, an object caught my attention out of the corner of my eye. On the counter was a brand new, top-of-the-line, green-handled dandelion puller. A treasure.

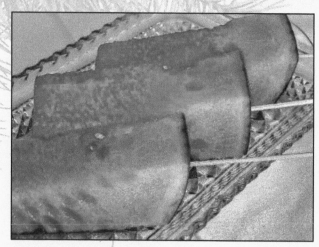

Watermelon Sicles

Slice a watermelon in half and place flat side down in serving bowl. Make slices 1½–2" apart in one direction. Turn watermelon and repeat in the other direction.

You will end up with popsicle-like pieces that guests can pull out with a toothpick.

This is literally a really neat way to eat this treat.

Chocolate-Covered Strawberries

INGREDIENTS

2 strawberries per person

Chocolate-flavored candy coating or almond bark (found in baking aisle)

White candy coating or almond bark

Paper or foil cups (liners)

DIRECTIONS

- Melt chocolate in small bowl in microwave, checking after one minute.
- 1 small square should cover a few strawberries.
- Stir chocolate until smooth and make sure all is melted.
- Dip washed and dried (pat dry) strawberry into chocolate.
- Place on parchment paper until dry.
- Melt small amount of white coating in microwave.
- Using small spoon, drip white coating onto chocolate-covered berry.
- Let dry and place in paper or foil cups.
- No need to refrigerate – but best eaten within a few hours.

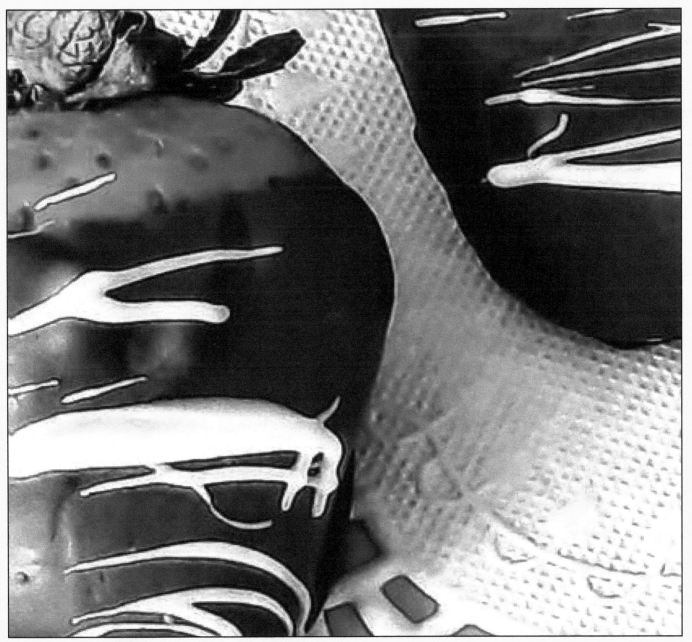

These are easy to make, elegant and delicious. Always a treat. No need to refrigerate unless room temperature is really warm.

23

Chocolate-Covered Nuts and Fruits

You can "chocolate-cover" almost anything you like. Here are some ideas:

- Dried fruits: Apricots, pineapple, pears. Melt chocolate as described in the Chocolate-Covered Strawberries recipe and dip fruits halfway into chocolate. Lay on parchment to dry.

- Grapes: For a tiny treat, use fresh grapes, wash and dry thoroughly before dipping

- Nuts: You can use walnuts, cashews, pecans, almonds, peanuts or other. Melt chocolate as described in strawberry recipe. Add nuts, or pieces if nuts are large, and stir until thoroughly coated. Spread nut/chocolate mixture on parchment and allow to harden for an hour or so. You can then drizzle a bit of melted white coating on top if desired. When completely hardened, break apart in pieces of desired size.

- Candies: Use your imagination. Crush peppermints (or buy them already crushed) and stir into melted chocolate as above. Another great combination is butterscotch and white chocolate ... the list goes on.

> *Always make sure the fruit is dry before dipping. Otherwise, the chocolate will not be smooth.*

A Little Salsa Humor

One family was getting ready to eat breakfast and I realized I had forgotten to put salsa out for the egg dish. I asked them if they were "salsa people." They said, "yes," then they laughed and told me their story. Their grandparents had started making salsa in their garage years back, and it became so famous that it was now a huge company.

The next morning, they brought me a jar from one of our local stores. The lid had a drawing of a woman on top - it was their grandmother. Yes, they were most definitely "salsa people."

These are as tasty as chocolate-covered strawberries. Bananas are always in season.

Chocolate-Covered Banana Bites

INGREDIENTS

Bananas: peel and slice into 1-inch bites

Chocolate flavored candy coating or almond bark (this comes in blocks in the baking aisle): one section (2 ounces) should be enough for 6-8 banana bites

White flavored candy coating or almond bark

Sprinkles

Small paper baking cups

DIRECTIONS

- Melt chocolate in small dish in microwave (check after 1 minute and continue until melted).
- Place bites in paper cups.
- Spoon melted chocolate over top of bites and spread so it runs down sides.
- Chocolate does not need to cover entire banana piece.
- Let cool for a few minutes.
- Melt small amount of white candy coating in microwave, checking after 1 minute.
- Carefully spoon small amount of white coating over top of each chocolate-covered bite.
- Immediately shake colored sprinkles on each bite.
- These should be left at room temperature unless it is really warm inside.
- They can be eaten as soon as chocolate coatings harden but can last a few hours as well. Best eaten within 3 hours of making them.

Je Langer, Je Besser

Round butter cookies with jam in the center

INGREDIENTS

3 cups flour

¾ cup sugar

2½ sticks butter (⅝ lb.)

1 grated lemon peel

4 egg yolks

Apricot Jam (or flavor of your choice)

INGREDIENTS (GLAZE)

¾ cup powdered sugar

1 Tablespoon lemon juice

1 Tablespoon water

DIRECTIONS

- Mix flour, sugar, butter and lemon peel by hand.
- Add egg yolks.
- Mix well by hand again. Dough will be fairly stiff.
- Roll into small balls, about the size of a large grape.
- Use finger in center of ball to make a depression.
- Fill with small amount of jam.
- Bake on ungreased pan @ 350F for approximately 20 minutes or until bottoms are very lightly browned.
- Mix glaze ingredients with spoon and brush on cookies after a few minutes of cooling.
- Move to cooling rack and cool completely before storing in an airtight container.
- Eat within a few days or freeze.
- These freeze very well and just need a few minutes sitting on the countertop to thaw.

My boys love these cookies. Of course, each one favored a different kind of jam; one apricot, one strawberry and one grape. My daughter stayed out of the vote.

Peanut Butter Cookies

Flourless – Gluten Free

INGREDIENTS

1 cup peanut butter

1 cup sugar

1 teaspoon vanilla

1 beaten egg

Coarse salt

DIRECTIONS

- Preheat oven to 400F.
- Mix peanut butter, sugar, vanilla and egg.
- Roll 1 Tablespoon dough into balls and place 1" apart on ungreased cookie sheet.
- Flatten just a bit with fork and sprinkle with coarse salt.
- Bake 5 minutes, turn cookie sheet around to bake evenly.
- Bake at least another 5 minutes, for a total of 10-15 minutes.
- Remove from oven when golden brown – do not over-bake.

These cookies are unbelievably easy and delicious – a favorite. Five simple ingredients ... doesn't get much easier than that.

Flip Days

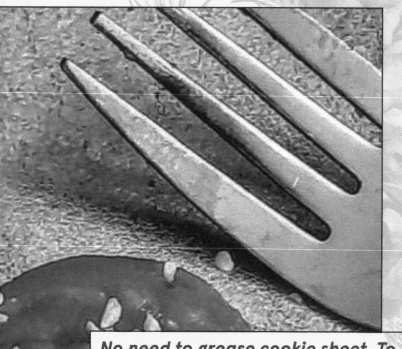

Speaking of easy, or not, what I called my flip days were anything but. They were downright chaotic.

This happened when I had a check-out and check-in on the same day. Most July days were like this, as were many others in the summer.

I remember wheeling the vacuum into the hall closet just as the doorbell rang.

Whew.

No need to grease cookie sheet. To keep dough from sticking to your hands, either wet your hands or "sugar" them and the dough should roll more smoothly. The baked cookies freeze very well after cooling, but they last several days out of freezer as long as they are tightly covered. (Dough does not freeze well, so bake them all.)

These cookies have a nice consistency and are really flavorful.

I like to welcome guests with some flavored water to accompany their afternoon treat. Some combinations of fruits and vegetables are quite tasty and add a twist to plain water. Cucumbers go well with lemon and lime. Just slice up as many as you'd like, add ice and cold water. Oranges add great flavor to water as well. They can be combined with lemon and strawberry slices to add additional color and flavor.

Beverages: So Many Choices

My friends are great...and they always bring me cute fox towels, fox mugs and fox knick-knacks. (They used to bring me chicken items before Fox Run B&B.) Much of what is in this photo was given to me by friends.

Kids always add fun to the mix. One family had two girls who thought the water was so good, they wanted me to enjoy it as well. They snuck upstairs, leaving "clue notes" for me, leading to where a glass of orange-flavored water was hiding. (Usually it was outside, right in the middle of the lawn.)

I always put out hot water along with the coffee for guests who enjoy tea or hot chocolate, or even cider. One family was here, and the husband told me his wife is a big tea drinker. I made sure to have a good selection of teas and plenty of hot water in the carafe. He got his coffee the next morning, sat down, looked at her with a quizzical expression on his face and asked, "You're drinking coffee? You never drink coffee!"

She said the coffee aroma sneaking down the stairs in the morning was so good that she had to have some. Be prepared. (Luckily, tea bags last a long time.)

Weddings: Go With the Flow

I hosted two weddings at the Bed & Breakfast. Wow, they were fun and intense! **I never knew so many people or so much food could fit into my kitchen.** Somehow it all got prepared and carried outside for the guests to enjoy.

I wore many hats those days, from parking attendant to tour guide to decorator to food assistant. What a great way to get to know a family and their friends while working together.

Have you ever had a Port-a-Potty placed in front of your home? Well, it was supposed to be off the yard in the trees. When I arrived home in enough time for the "scheduled" drop off, it had already been deposited smack dab in front of the B&B, right in the center of the front circle for all coming up the drive to see.

Needless to say, that's where it stayed throughout the wedding. (I know my limits.)

It turned out that we had a few more guests than originally anticipated (i.e., twice as many, to be exact).

**Beautiful people.
Beautiful day.**

Main Breakfast Dishes

Crepe Concoctions

My family used to call crepes "pala-chinke," and yes, you can find these online. They look just like our crepes, but ours may taste better.

We traditionally had crepes for dinner, not breakfast. They were served after soup, oftentimes Matzo Ball Soup. We would sprinkle cinnamon and sugar over them – or spread jam on them and roll them up. Some would pour syrup on top as well.

When I started the B&B, I would make them as described in this recipe, with cream cheese filling and folded into triangles for breakfast.

They are great with either strawberry sauce, syrup or chocolate sauce over them, and newly-discovered Loganberry Syrup from Washington State. (Thanks Tyler & Jenna.)

I once asked my kids the best way to eat crepes and I received four different answers. One said, "Cinnamon and sugar is the best." Another said "jam," while another said "Nutella." The fourth said, "Everything together."

There you have it, the Tyler, Holly, Alex and Cody preferred ways of topping their crepes.

This is the size pan I use for crepes (6"–7" across bottom). The batter should just cover the bottom.

This recipe makes about 20 crepes and feeds 4–6 guests when serving other dishes alongside.

Pairing options – bacon, sausage, yogurt bar, fried potatoes, muffins.

Crepes

Sauces and Toppings: Syrup, chocolate sauce or strawberry sauce are great. For strawberry sauce, blend 2 cups of fresh strawberries and add a teaspoon or two of sugar to taste, or buy frozen strawberries with sugar, thaw and blend at high speed.

INGREDIENTS (CREPE)

4 eggs

8 Tablespoons sugar

½ teaspoon salt

1½ cups milk

1 teaspoon vanilla

1¼ cups flour

INGREDIENTS (FILLING)

6 oz. cream cheese

2 Tablespoons sour cream

2 Tablespoons sugar

1 teaspoon vanilla

DIRECTIONS (CREPE)

- Blend all ingredients until smooth (blender or whisk).
- Grease small (6-7" bottom) skillet with butter.
- Using ladle or measuring cup, pour about ¼ cup batter into pan.
- Tilt pan continuously until batter covers bottom of pan.
- Cook on medium heat and flip when barely brown (30 seconds – 1 minute).
- Using plastic spatula, gently pick up crepe and flip.
- At first sign of browning, flip onto cooling rack.

DIRECTIONS (CREAM CHEESE FILLING)

- Spread each crepe thinly with filling.
- Fold crepe in half and then in half again.
- Arrange on platter and cover tightly.
- Can be refrigerated overnight, if desired, or served fresh.
- Keep covered and heat for about 15 minutes in 350F oven just before serving.

Crepes are like anything else – once you know how to make them, they are not difficult. Pouring batter into the pan while at the same time tipping and twirling the pan to get an even coating is kind of like ... patting your head and rubbing your stomach. Once you've practiced and mastered it, piece of cake, right?

This is what the crepes look like, plain, after removing from pan.

Opas, Bikes and Warm Milk

Funny how some memories are so vivid, and when you mention them, others say, "I don't remember that at all." Apparently, I'm the only one who loved eating corn flakes with warm milk. The best! ... or maybe I loved it because my grandpa made it. It was our favorite meal to eat together. You want some now, don't you?

The breakfast must have given us great energy. My grandpa (Opa) ran next to me on my new blue two-wheeler, and I was pedaling as fast as a 5-year-old could! I turned to yell, "We're going really fast!" He wasn't there. I saw him standing two blocks back ... I immediately fell over.

Ascension Tree – Northern El Paso County

Culturally Modified Trees

Ute Healing Tree

The Culturally Modified Tree on the previous page is an Ascension Tree located in northern El Paso County. It is a Native American memorial tree possibly signifying the cycle of birth, life and walking on. The Association for Native American Sacred Trees and Places (NASTaP) was started in February 2018 to spread awareness and foster preservation of these trees and places.

There are many Culturally Modified Trees in El Paso County, throughout Colorado, in most US states and throughout Canada. Former El Paso County Sheriff, John Wesley Anderson, has published two books on these trees with the guidance of Dr. James Jefferson, President of NASTaP and a Ute elder from the Southern Ute Reservation, Ignacio, CO.

Southwest Casserole

INGREDIENTS

2 large or 3 small wheat or white tortillas

1 cup ham, turkey, sausage (chopped/crumbled)

2 cups grated cheese (Colby Jack or mixed)

One small can diced green chiles, mild

⅛ teaspoon each of salt, pepper, cumin, garlic, onion powder

3 eggs

3 Tablespoons milk

Small tomato/bell pepper

Hungarian Paprika

DIRECTIONS

- Grease bottom and sides of pie plate with butter.
- Using a small amount of oil or butter, on medium heat, lightly brown each tortilla on both sides in skillet.
- Cut tortillas in strips, maybe ½" wide.
- Using same pan, lightly brown sausages and slice into small pieces.
- Layer in pie plate - half of the tortilla strips, half of the chiles, half of the sausage pieces and half of the cheese (1 cup) – repeat layers.
- Whisk or shake eggs, milk and spices and pour over layers in pie plate.
- Slice tomatoes or peppers and arrange on top.
- Sprinkle with paprika.
- Cover tightly and chill overnight in fridge.
- Bake uncovered @ 350F for approximately 45 minutes.
- Done when set to touch and golden brown.
- Let cool 10 minutes or so before slicing.

Serve with sour cream and salsa on the side. Paired with fried potatoes, bread and a fruit dish, this will fuel you for a hike or bike ride.

These are baked in muffin tins ... simple and quick to prepare. They were originally called "Eggs in a Pig Pen" and made with bacon, but that made them greasy. I switched the meat to turkey, but then the name had to change. (The pigs were happy about that.)

One guest, Jolie, suggested "Egg Pillows." I kind of liked that.

Egg Pillows

Simple, delicious and look nice on a platter.

INGREDIENTS (EACH TIN)

1 egg

1 slice of deli turkey

½ teaspoon butter

2 teaspoons cream (Half-and-Half)

Salt & pepper

DIRECTIONS

- Thoroughly grease muffin tins with butter.
- Place turkey slice in each tin. Each slice should cover bottom and come up sides.
- Crack 1 egg into each tin over turkey.
- Place ½ teaspoon butter in each.
- Pour 2 teaspoons cream over each.
- Sprinkle with salt and pepper.
- Bake @ 350F for approximately 15 minutes.
- Low broil for approximately 5 minutes, a little more or less depending on doneness desired. Watch closely.
- Cut around each one with knife and spoon out onto serving dish.

Some dishes and flavors just go together, like the old ice cream commercials. They just knew the flavors to mix. Breakfasts are much like this.

Certain items sound and taste good together, like Egg Pillows, Bacon and Chocolate Pound Cake.

Great Danes to Chipmunks

I'll never forget the young couple from Ohio; they drove all the way in a Subaru with their two great Danes who were sisters. They looked like ponies loping up the steps for breakfast. Their heads grazed the counter where all the food was set. They could have easily finished it off, especially a platter of egg pillows, in no time, but they had manners. Thank goodness.

*In Colorado, foods cool quickly, so keeping them covered is important. Warming the serving plates in the oven helps as well (my neighbor Rob taught me this). Also, in our drier climate, **keeping** **foods wrapped tightly is crucial** to keeping them fresh.*

While growing up in Ohio it was equally crucial for different reasons.

One summer day my mom had baked a cheesecake. My brother had friends over and there were some chipmunk shenanigans. The little critter got loose and disappeared. The next day we prepared to serve the cheesecake. Surprise! The little guy had apparently taken a run across the sweet field of our dessert. P.S. We ate it anyways. The little paw prints were pretty cute.

Fall is a beautiful time in Colorado. This photo was taken at the upper pond, Fox Run Park, a 15-minute walk from the B&B.

This recipe was given to me by my 96-year-old neighbor who said it freezes well after being baked. She's right. You can just bake, freeze, pop it in the oven until warm and serve – voila. One variation could be 2 cups swiss and 1 cup cooked bacon, or any other combo you'd like to try ... the spicier the meat, the less spicy the cheese needs to be.

Quiche with Hash Brown Crust

INGREDIENTS

24 oz. frozen shredded hash browns, thawed

¼ cup butter, melted (½ stick)

1 cup diced cooked ham, Canadian bacon or sausage

1 cup grated pepper-jack cheese

1 cup grated swiss cheese

½ cup cream (Half-and-Half)

2 eggs

½ teaspoon seasoned salt

DIRECTIONS (CRUST)

- Preheat oven @ 425F.
- Grease a 10" quiche dish or pie plate.
- Squeeze thawed hash browns between paper towels to eliminate moisture.
- Press hash browns in dish to form even layer on bottom and sides.
- Brush with the melted butter, covering all edges.
- Bake 25 minutes, remove from oven and cool.
- If preparing crust ahead of time, cool, cover and refrigerate. Otherwise, fill as directed below.

DIRECTIONS (FILLING)

- Decrease oven temp to 350F.
- Layer ham or sausage over crust.
- Sprinkle cheeses over meat.
- In small bowl, beat together Half-and-Half, eggs and salt.
- Pour over cheeses and bake uncovered for 30-40 minutes and until center is set or knife comes out clean.

Apple Sausage Quiche

INGREDIENTS

One 9" pie crust - either homemade or store-bought/frozen

4 oz. pork sausage (spicy or not)

½ cup milk

1½ large eggs or 2 small/medium (if doubling recipe use 3 eggs)

¼ cup mayonnaise

1 Tablespoon flour

1 cup shredded cheese (I use a Colby/Jack or mixed blend)

1 small/medium granny smith apple, chopped

DIRECTIONS

- Use a regular pie plate for this dish. It does not need to be deep.
- Prick bottom and sides of pie crust - Bake @ 400F for 6 minutes.
- Brown sausage on stove, breaking into crumbles while cooking.
- Drain extra grease.
- Whisk together milk, eggs, mayo and flour.
- Stir in sausage, cheese and chopped apple.
- Spoon mixture into pie crust - sprinkle with salt and pepper.
- Bake @ 400F for 40-45 minutes until light brown.

Apples in recipes ... many times the recipe calls for peeling the apples. Ugh, who wants to peel an apple, right? Seriously, why would you peel away nutrition? I think the peels give the dish extra flavor and texture, so I always leave them on.

This quiche has a unique, mildly spicy flavor without any added spices. I think it's a combination of sausage and Granny Smith apple. Delicious!

You won't believe how easy and quick this is to prepare. Colorful and delicious eaten right after baking, but good out of the fridge as well.

Breakfast Pizza

Who doesn't want pizza for breakfast?

INGREDIENTS

Pastry for single crust 9" pie - either homemade or store-bought. I purchase the frozen crusts that are rolled up, 2 to a package, and like having them readily available in my freezer.

½ pound bacon, cooked and crumbled

2 cups (8 oz.) grated swiss cheese

4 eggs

1⅓ cups sour cream

2 Tablespoons dried parsley (use a little more if parsley is fresh)

DIRECTIONS (CRUST)

- Roll out pastry a little larger than a 12" round pizza pan (I use the pan with holes).
- Fit pastry in pan, fold outside edge so it's double thickness and press with thumb/fingers to make finished edge.
- Bake crust on lower oven rack @ 425F for 5 minutes.
- Remove from oven.

DIRECTIONS (FILLING/BAKING)

- Sprinkle cooked bacon and cheese over crust.
- Whisk together eggs and sour cream. Pour over crust evenly.
- Top with sliced tomatoes and colorful sweet peppers (red, orange, yellow).
- Sprinkle parsley over the top.
- Bake on lower rack @ 425F for 20-25 minutes until barely beginning to brown.
- Remove from oven and let sit 5 minutes before slicing into wedges with pizza cutter.

Spinach Sun-Dried Tomato Quiche

Tasty ... Healthy ... Yum.

INGREDIENTS

1 frozen/refrigerated pie crust

⅔ large red onion, cut into rings

1 cup fresh spinach

1 Tablespoon butter

4 eggs

1 cup milk

¼ teaspoon each salt and pepper

¼ teaspoon basil

¼ cup black olives

½ cup sun-dried tomatoes, sliced

1 cup shredded swiss cheese

DIRECTIONS

- Open pie dough, roll out a bit larger than pie plate and place in plate.
- Double over outside edge and pinch or use fork to form pattern.
- Bake crust per directions on package.
- Fry onion and spinach with butter, then scoop mixture into baked crust.
- Whisk eggs, milk, salt, pepper and basil; pour over spinach/onion in crust.
- Top with olives, sun-dried tomatoes and cheese.
- Bake @ 350F for 35-40 minutes.

This Spinach Sun-Dried Tomato Quiche is so simple, quick to prepare and bake, and very flavorful. No need to make the night before – you can easily do this one in the morning. You can experiment with different cheeses – swiss, Jarlsberg or other.

Dutch Baby

Apple & Cinnamon

INGREDIENTS

1 large gala apple, thinly sliced

1 Tablespoon sugar

3 Tablespoons butter, divided

2 large eggs

½ cup milk (low fat/fat free)

½ cup flour, sifted

½ teaspoon cinnamon

¼ teaspoon salt

¼ teaspoon nutmeg

Powdered sugar for garnish

INGREDIENTS (TOPPING)

½ cup sour cream

¼ cup brown sugar

1 to 2 Tablespoons apple/orange juice

DIRECTIONS

- Preheat oven to 450F.
- Toss apple slices with sugar in bowl.
- Melt one Tablespoon butter in skillet.
- Add apples to skillet and sauté 3-5 minutes.
- Whisk eggs and milk in bowl.
- Whisk in flour, cinnamon, salt and nutmeg.
- Melt remaining 2 Tablespoons butter in separate skillet or pie plate.
- Immediately pour egg mixture in hot dish.
- Top with cooked apples.
- Bake approximately 20 minutes until puffed/golden.
- Sprinkle with powdered sugar and serve topping on the side.

DIRECTIONS (TOPPING)

- Stir together sour cream and brown sugar.
- Microwave 45 seconds.
- Whisk until sugar dissolves.
- Stir in juice one Tablespoon at a time.

Dutch Baby is last-minute, meaning it should be made in the morning and eaten right after removing from oven. Also, it serves 2-3 people, so you might want to make two recipes. Definitely serve with the topping – a must.

If you sauté the apples in a cast-iron skillet, you can remove them when done and complete the recipe in the same skillet, which can go in the oven. It turns out a bit differently every time. In Colorado we like to blame that on elevation or lack of humidity. However, it is always good!

Refrigerator's Cold; Is Oven Hot?

Speaking of ovens, I learned many new skills while running the Bed & Breakfast. Early on in the business, I was preparing breakfast at O-dark thirty and I had a sense my oven was not as hot as it should be. It was simply not heating properly.

After a brief panic, I debated walking the woods to Rob and Jeff's with my unbaked batter or first calling my friend Linda, who is an early riser. I went with the "early riser" idea.

Thank goodness she was there (of course, where else would she be at that time?) and I drove the batter, in pans, over to her house and baked everything. I was able to serve the breakfast and I don't think my guests even knew what had happened. In my mind that was not information that would be helpful to their B&B experience.

Sure enough, the heating element in my oven had gone out. I found out how simple it was to install a new one. The challenge was finding the proper one.

This wood burner sat in the main living area of the B&B. It was a favorite sitting area for guests ... warm, cozy and relaxing. It was even used throughout the summer for heating up those chilly nights or roasting marshmallows if it were raining and the outdoor firepit couldn't be used. In the winter, this was the warmest spot in the house.

Schmarrn

This dish has many names ... I won't even attempt to spell some of them ... but no matter how you slice it (or fry it), it is basically fried dough. Oh, and it's good. Really, really good.

INGREDIENTS

⅓ cup cream of wheat (farina)

1⅓ cups milk

½ teaspoon salt

5 egg yolks

1½ cups flour

1 teaspoon baking powder

5 egg whites

5 Tablespoons sugar

⅓ cup oil

DIRECTIONS

- Soak cream of wheat (farina) in milk approximately 1 hour (room temp).
- Add salt and egg yolks.
- Beat with fork until blended.
- Add flour and baking powder – beat until smooth.
- Beat egg whites at high speed until stiff.
- Add sugar 1 Tablespoon at a time.
- Fold egg white/sugar mixture into batter.
- Heat oil in frying pan. (I cheat and use less oil, but that's just me. I sense my kids rolling their eyes right now.)
- Pour batter in and cook, breaking dough apart with spoon or spatula as it's cooking.
- Serve with cinnamon/sugar or syrup, any flavor.

Serve Schmarrn with syrup, cinnamon/sugar and a side of fruit

The strata recipe serves 6-8. For a gluten-free dish use sliced corn tortillas instead of English muffins.

Spinach or Asparagus (Overnight) Strata

INGREDIENTS

2 cups fresh spinach, chopped, or 1 pound fresh asparagus cut into 1" pieces

4 English muffins - split and toasted

2 cups (8 oz.) shredded co-jack cheese, divided (any orange & white mixed)

1 cup diced cooked ham or other meat (turkey deli meat, sausage, etc.)

½ cup chopped red pepper or tomato

8 eggs

2 cups milk

1 teaspoon salt

1 teaspoon ground mustard

¼ teaspoon pepper

DIRECTIONS

- Grease a 13" x 9" x 2" baking dish, glass or other.
- Bring 8 cups water to boil, add asparagus and cook 3 minutes.
- Drain and place in ice water briefly.
- Drain and pat dry.
- If using spinach, it does not need to be cooked. Wash and pat dry.
- Toast English muffin halves and arrange cut side up in baking dish.
- Cut halves in smaller pieces if necessary, to fill in spaces.
- Sprinkle with 1 cup cheese, all asparagus or spinach, meat and pepper/tomato.
- Whisk together eggs, milk, salt, mustard and pepper. Pour gently into dish.
- Cover tightly and refrigerate overnight.
- Remove from fridge 30 minutes before baking and sprinkle with remaining 1 cup cheese.
- Bake uncovered @ 375F for 40-45 minutes or until toothpick comes out clean. Cool 5 minutes before cutting.

Strata is versatile – you can please many palates with ham, tur-key, sausage or other meats.

Make sure to sprinkle ingredients evenly into dish to make for an attractive presentation.

This is perfect for holidays or brunches with its splash of color.

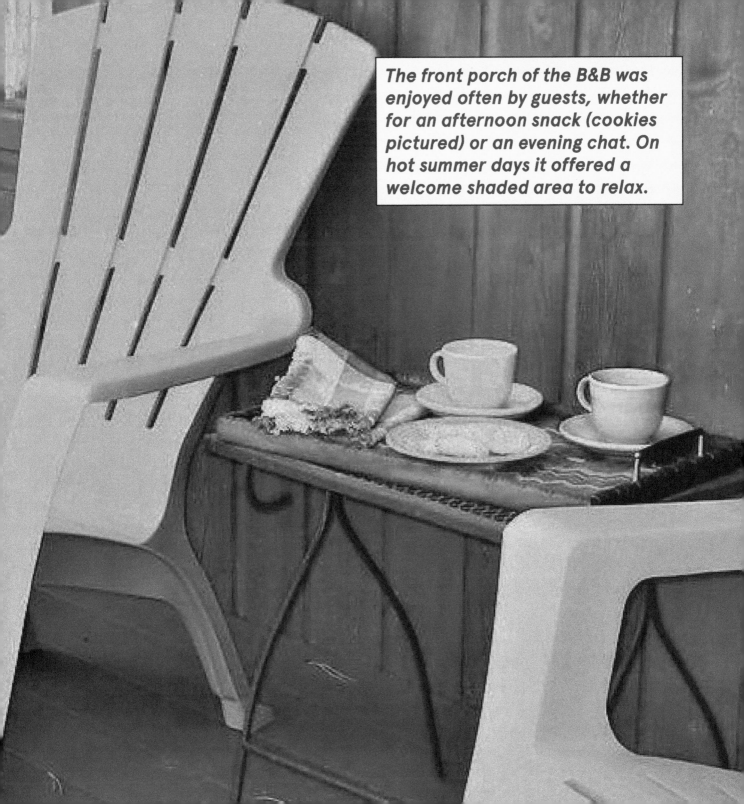

The front porch of the B&B was enjoyed often by guests, whether for an afternoon snack (cookies pictured) or an evening chat. On hot summer days it offered a welcome shaded area to relax.

Character Building at Sanborn

Laura and Sandy Sanborn started Sanborn Western Camps in the 1950's and were very memorable human beings. Sandy tooled around in his powder-blue Beetle Bug and if he saw you nearing the end of a job (or being idle, heaven forbid), he charmingly persuaded you into doing another "little something" like creosoting fenceposts or some similar endearing task. He seemed to know just when to show up.

Laura was charming as well ... and when I first started there, she had the entire female staff up to her house on the hill. As we sat on the chairs, couches and floor of her living room, we received an introduction and welcome to camp, and also had the chance to introduce ourselves. She made us feel at home and welcome. Those were the "good old days."

Jane, on the other hand, RAN the girls camp, High Trails, with an amazing amount of efficiency. She had a wicked sense of humor, a sharp mind that held an incredible amount of information, and an uncanny sense of organization. She knew when to delegate and trust you with a job, trip or whatever it was you were (supposed to be) doing ... but was always approachable for advice. Sometimes we were amazed how she always seemed to know "what happened" before we even got back to tell her (or confess).

Speaking of camp, lots of friends and wonderful memories resulted from my camp experience. One of my co-counselors those first years, Laurie, is still a close friend to this day, and yes, we laugh at those "camp stories" still so close to our hearts, including fabricating articles for local newspapers, performing goldfish burials, learning how to handle wild ferrets with a leather glove, figuring out how to extract the barnyard animals which were "displaced" in your vehicle ... the list goes on.

More Sanborn Character Building

Pete and Donna mentored me in horsemanship and equine care, and Jerry ran the boys' camp with an amazing amount of calm while still having time to help us out when needed. My co-wrangler Jean and I would sneak out during rest periods to race our horses down the path ... good times. (Pete and Donna – ignore that last line.) We always tried to beat the guy wrangler to get the best old truck, shifting on the column – we called it the Wrangler Wagon. Mike, Carolyn, Chip and Rob, you will remember this.

Some of those memories were of food ... rip and tear bread our bakery would make (darn, don't have that recipe!), brown bread out of a can eaten while on long horse trips, drinking boiling water when no food was left and the most memorable was passing around a raw onion on the last night of a trip, only because that was the only food item remaining.

Whew - makes me appreciate this quiche even more!

This quiche recipe came from the owner of an outdoor camp I worked at when I first arrived in Colorado ... and is one of the first recipes I acquired while living here. It has been baked and eaten for over 40 years and is good every time! For a little variety, sauté some fresh spinach for a few minutes and place over crust before adding other ingredients.

Laura's Quiche

INGREDIENTS

2 baked pie crusts

8 strips bacon, cooked and crumbled

2 cups swiss or mozzarella cheese
(or one cup of each), grated

4 eggs

1 cup milk

1 cup whipping cream

½ teaspoon salt

¼ teaspoon pepper

¼ teaspoon nutmeg

2 cans French Fried Onions

2 Tablespoons chives

3 drops Tabasco (optional)

DIRECTIONS

- Prick pie shells with fork - bake 8 minutes at temp on crust directions.
- Sprinkle cheese and bacon over crusts.
- Beat eggs, milk, cream and spices.
- Cut through onions while still in cans.
- Pour egg mixture over cheese and bacon in both shells.
- Press dried onion pieces into mixture with fork.
- Bake @ 350F for 30-40 minutes.

Oatmeal (Baked)

Quick prep time and simple to put together. Serves 4-6.

INGREDIENTS

1½ cups 2% milk

1 egg

½ cup plain/vanilla yogurt or applesauce

1 teaspoon vanilla

2 Tablespoons brown sugar

3 cups oats (reg or quick)

2 teaspoons cinnamon

2 cups fruit (2 varieties; choose from raspberries, blueberries, blackberries, strawberries, peaches)

Walnut/pecan pieces

DIRECTIONS

- Preheat oven to 350F.
- Grease 8" x 8" glass or ceramic baking dish.
- Combine milk, egg, yogurt, vanilla, brown sugar, oatmeal and cinnamon.
- Add ¾ of the above mixture to the baking dish and spread evenly.
- Layer fruit evenly on top of mixture in pan (and nuts if desired).
- Top with remaining ¼ oatmeal mixture.
- Bake for 30 minutes or until bubbly.
- Pour a few Tablespoons cream or milk over dish after removing from oven.
- Cut into rectangular or square sections and serve in bowls.
- Top with a bit more milk/cream or warm syrup (yum).

Even non-oatmeal lovers usually love this. It's that good! The syrup really adds flavor, and the cream keeps it, well ... creamy.

Healthy breakfast ... healthy people ... brings to mind a group of three women who brought three healthy dogs as well! They had traveled from different states to participate in an Agility Workshop in the Black Forest.

One of the great benefits of being a dog-friendly B&B is that I had people from all over bring their pets, and I wouldn't have had the opportunity to meet them otherwise. It was definitely a BONUS.

This strata has a different flair – it is very good, but make sure your guests like salmon. I would serve this more for a brunch than an early breakfast.

Bagels and Lox Strata

INGREDIENTS

¼ cup butter, melted

8 cups cubed bagels (4-6 bagels)

3 ounces smoked salmon, cut into small pieces

2 cups shredded swiss cheese

¼ cup fresh chives

8 eggs, lightly beaten

2 cups milk

1 cup cottage cheese

¼ teaspoon black pepper

¼ teaspoon dill

DIRECTIONS

- Pour melted butter in 9"x13" baking dish.
- Arrange bagel pieces and sprinkle with salmon.
- Top with swiss cheese and chives.
- Whisk eggs, milk, cottage cheese, pepper and dill.
- Pour over dish and press down with spoon.
- Refrigerate at least 2 hours and up to 24 hours.
- Bake uncovered @ 350F for 45 minutes.
- Cool slightly and cut into squares.

Tolerance of Intolerances

One of the standard questions I asked when receiving a booking was "Any food allergies or intolerances?" Definitely important information for a B&B owner to have.

Gluten and dairy were fairly simple to work around, using almond, rice and tapioca flours as well as almond, coconut, soy or lactose-free milk.

Some of the more interesting and unique requests were no truffle oil (no worries), no raw potatoes (again...no worries), keto diet (there go my crepes), and just plain "don't care for tomatoes, cucumbers and peppers." Ahh, my garnishes!

My favorite, however, was an entire family who was lactose intolerant. Upon arrival they announced, "We want to eat everything and will just take a Lactaid pill every morning." Works for me.

Lactaid pills became a staple at the beverage bar.

The greens and blooms of summer

Breads & Beyond

This bread is a favorite of mine. It has that flavor that will stay with you and have your guests wanting more.

The chopped nuts enhance it even further.

It pairs wonderfully with any egg dish. It is also perfect for an afternoon snack served with coffee or tea.

Orange Cranberry Bread

Makes one loaf – so easy and tasty. This bread is made with less butter and contains orange juice. It is almost better after sitting a while, well-wrapped, even overnight.

INGREDIENTS

2 cups flour

¼ teaspoon salt

½ teaspoon baking soda

1 cup sugar

1 egg, beaten

2 Tablespoons butter, melted

¾ cup orange juice

1 cup cranberries

¾ cup chopped nuts if desired (cashews, walnuts, almonds, pecans)

DIRECTIONS

- Stir together flour, salt, baking soda and sugar.
- Add the beaten egg, melted butter and orange juice.
- Mix well.
- Stir in cranberries and nuts.
- Bake @ 325F in a greased, lined (parchment) loaf pan for 1 hour.
- Remove from oven and immediately brush with butter.
- Cool at least half an hour before removing from pan.

Apple Cake

INGREDIENTS

1½ cups flour

1 cup sugar

1 teaspoon baking powder

½ teaspoon baking soda

¼ teaspoon salt

1 egg

½ cup milk

1 teaspoon vanilla

½ cup melted butter

4 medium granny smith apples

INGREDIENTS (TOPPING)

¼ cup flour

¼ cup butter

½ cup brown sugar (firmly packed)

DIRECTIONS

- Preheat oven to 350F.
- Grease 8" x 8" square (glass or other) pan.
- Stir flour, sugar, baking powder, baking soda and salt.
- Form a well in center and add the lightly beaten egg.
- Add milk, vanilla and melted butter to well and stir thoroughly.
- Quarter apples and slice out core area - slice quarters into thin wedges.
- Stir apples into batter and pour into pan, spreading evenly.
- Mix topping ingredients and sprinkle evenly over cake.
- Bake 35-45 minutes or until top of cake springs back when lightly touched. If cake is browning too quickly, lay a piece of foil loosely on top near the end of baking time.

This cake is a crowd pleaser and freezes well, but it is usually eaten before making it to the freezer.

I knew there were several different types of apples: Granny Smith, Gala, Pink Lady, Honey Crisp, Red Delicious, Golden Delicious, McIntosh, Jonathan and a few others. Well, come to find out, there are 2500+ different kinds grown just in the US alone, and possibly 7500 in the world. Sheesh, that's a lot of apple trees.

Autumn and Horror Films

Apples, pumpkins and other autumn harvests remind me of many fall guests. Jim and Patty returned several times on their visits from Nebraska, and their wonderful gift of a ceramic pumpkin plug-in (with choice of wax scents) is a seasonal reminder of the special breakfasts and conversations we shared.

Another fall visit was from a group of film school students. This was a "first time ever!" Three of them, plus one parent, stayed over for the weekend ...but the days were filled with 30+ students doing make-up, sound, lights, directing and acting. It was non-stop and very lively!

My B&B was turned into a stage with the theme being a spoof on horror films. Think goblins and spirits emerging from the forest, torture chambers in the barn and ghost children on the swing set. Yes, it was pretty convincing. The great culmination was getting to see the finished product at their film festival. They titled it, "**THE CABIN**." It definitely put a unique twist on how the B&B was used.

One guest made a point of saying during breakfast, "This apricot jam is REALLY good on the poppy bread!" When a guest says something like that, I pay attention.

Poppy Seed Bread

Makes 2 loaves and freezes well. If you don't have quite enough poppy seeds, less will work.

INGREDIENTS

3⅓ cups flour

5 eggs

2 cups sugar

1¾ cups milk

1¼ cups poppy seeds

1 cup oil

1½ Tablespoons baking powder

1½ teaspoons almond extract

DIRECTIONS

- Combine flour, sugar, poppy seeds and baking powder.
- Beat eggs and add milk, oil and almond extract.
- Add above to dry ingredients and stir until smooth.
- Pour into 2 greased, floured and paper-lined loaf pans.
- Bake @ 350F for 50-60 minutes.
- Cool in pan for 30-60 minutes and then remove from pans and place breads on rack to complete cooling.

Baking with poppyseed always reminds me of Christmas, but of course this bread is great any time of the year.

Aromatic ... delicious ... moist ... will make your entire house smell wonderful.

Makes 2 loaves ... if you only want chopped nuts in one loaf, wait until batter is in bread pan to add nuts and then mix in gently. This way you will please every palate.

Pumpkin Bread

INGREDIENTS

3 cups sugar

3½ cups flour

1 teaspoon baking powder

2 teaspoons baking soda

1 teaspoon salt

4 eggs

1 teaspoon ground cloves

1 teaspoon ground cinnamon

¾ cup oil

1 cup water

2 cups canned pumpkin

1 cup chopped nuts (walnuts, pecans)

DIRECTIONS

- Mix dry ingredients (sugar, flour, baking powder, baking soda, salt, cloves and cinnamon).
- Add eggs, oil, water, pumpkin. Mix well with mixer or by hand.
- Stir in chopped nuts.
- Place in 2 greased, floured and paper-lined loaf pans.
- Bake @ 325F for approximately 1 hour or until pick inserted in center of loaves comes out clean.
- If browning too quickly, loosely place foil over bread in last 15 minutes of baking.
- Freezes very well.

This cake is a crowd pleaser but is usually completely consumed before making it to the freezer.

For a tasty spread on this Chocolate Pound Cake, mix a can of blueberry pie filling and a can of cranberry sauce.

Lemon pie filling (custard), which is found in the baking aisle of the grocery store, is also a wonderful pairing (pictured). If you really want to get fancy, beat some whipping cream and add a teaspoon of almond flavoring.

Chocolate Sour Cream Pound Cake

INGREDIENTS

1 cup butter

2 cups sugar

1 cup brown sugar

6 eggs

2½ cups flour

¼ teaspoon baking soda

½ cup baking cocoa

8 oz. sour cream

2 teaspoons vanilla

DIRECTIONS

- Preheat oven to 325F.
- Beat butter, add sugar & brown sugar, blend well.
- Add eggs and beat well.
- Combine soda, flour, cocoa.
- Add dry ingredients above to creamed mixture, alternating with sour cream.
- Stir in vanilla.
- Put in greased/floured 10" tube pan.
- Bake @ 325F for 80 minutes.
- Recipe can be halved and baked in loaf pan.

Dogs and Disappearing Chocolate

I'm not sure what percentage of people prefers chocolate over other flavors, but I know one thing: people LOVE chocolate. One of my families who came for a three-week visit was among those.

Brigitte, Maurice, Emma and Dickens (the wonder dog) checked in for a visit, and they soon became friends. We would hike together, visit over meals and talk of their possible move to Colorado.

Even Dickens, the Beagle/Pointer mix, was enthusiastic! In fact, he worked his way through the dog gate at the top of the stairs in all his excitement. My dog, Jesse, thought this was great.

Luckily, Maurice was handy with mesh fencing and tools, but eventually we just kept the gate open.

To accommodate their working schedule, we often ended up preparing dinners instead of breakfasts. The day that brownies (another chocolate treat) were waiting on the counter for dessert, our beagle Todd thought he would show his appreciation by helping himself to some. Our other dog who was older and showed much more restraint, Zeb, just rolled his eyes with a "There he goes again" look.

My guests got a little less chocolate that day.

P.S. The family moved out here the next year.

Elder Wisdom: Take a Break

The Applesauce Nut Bread on the following pages was a favorite of my neighbor and good friend, Harriette. She lived a great long life and passed away just before her 99th birthday.

She was always delighted when I would bring extra B&B food down the road to her home, sometimes on a tray with all the fixings. Harriette would rave about the topping on this bread - how delicious it was!

Although always a huge supporter of my business, she did have her moments where her voice would get stern and serious, and I would hear the lecture on working too hard without taking a break.

A glass of wine was her favorite kind of break. I miss her presence and her young spirit.

This bread is very flavorful in a cinnamon-kind-of-way. It is high, light and moist. It goes well with an egg dish of any kind. It is also a great snack with coffee, tea or hot cider.

What Happens in the Woods Stays in the Woods

Applesauce Nut Bread

INGREDIENTS

1 cup sugar

1 cup unsweetened applesauce

⅓ cup oil

1 teaspoon baking soda

½ teaspoon baking powder

½ teaspoon cinnamon

2 eggs

3 teaspoons milk

2 cups flour

¼ teaspoon salt

¼ teaspoon nutmeg

¾ cup chopped nuts (any variety)

TOPPING

¼ cup brown sugar

¼ cup chopped nuts

¼ teaspoon cinnamon

DIRECTIONS

- Combine sugar, applesauce, oil, eggs and milk.
- Mix together flour, soda, baking powder, cinnamon, salt and nutmeg.
- Add above to applesauce mixture.
- Stir in nuts.
- Put into well-greased, floured and lined loaf pan (line with parchment paper).
- Combine topping ingredients and sprinkle over batter.
- Bake @ 350F for 1 hour.
- Cap loosely with foil after 30 minutes to prevent over-browning.

Blueberry Crunch Cake

INGREDIENTS

1½ cups flour

¾ cup sugar

1 Tablespoon baking powder

½ teaspoon salt

¼ teaspoon nutmeg

⅓ cup butter, firm

1 cup blueberries

⅓ cup milk

1 teaspoon vanilla

1 egg

INGREDIENTS (TOPPING)

½ cup chopped walnuts

½ cup brown sugar

2 Tablespoons flour

2 teaspoons cinnamon

2 Tablespoons butter, melted

DIRECTIONS

- Mix topping ingredients - place half into greased and floured tube pan.
- In large bowl stir flour, sugar, baking powder, salt and nutmeg.
- With 2 knives or pastry blender, cut in butter until coarse crumbs.
- Gently stir in blueberries.
- Beat egg with milk and vanilla - add to mixture, stirring just until combined.
- Spread half of batter on top of topping in pan.
- Add remaining topping and remaining batter.
- Bake @ 350F for 45-60 minutes. Let cool approximately 20 minutes.
- Cut into wedges and sprinkle with powdered sugar.

A mixture of crunchy, crumbly and very flavorful, this also freezes well. It can be prepared the day before, but make sure it is covered - airtight.

Lemon Rosemary Muffins

Gluten Free

INGREDIENTS

1½ cups rice flour (or other gluten-free flour)

1 teaspoon sea salt or coarse salt

1 teaspoon baking soda

4 eggs

½ cup honey

½ cup oil

2 Tablespoons fresh rosemary, chopped (can substitute dry – 1 Tablespoon)

2 Tablespoons lemon zest (grated fresh lemon peel)

DIRECTIONS

- In a large bowl, combine flour, salt and baking soda.
- Add eggs, honey, oil, rosemary and lemon peel.
- Spoon into 12 paper-lined muffin tins.
- Bake @ 350F for approximately 15 minutes.
- Remove from oven when toothpick comes out clean.
- If desired, brush muffins with melted butter while they are still warm.

These muffins are very light and flavorful.

I love keeping a live rosemary plant in the house. It doesn't require a very large pot, and the fresh herb smells so wonderful!

Even during the winter, you can have fresh rosemary at your fingertips.

Speaking of winter, or weather ... one of the adventures of living in Colorado is never knowing what to expect with the weather. My actual conversation with a guest scheduled to arrive at my B&B the end of March is on the following page.

Crocus ... our first wildflower of spring.

Does Colorado Have Spring?

Phone rings.

Hello, Fox Run Bed and Breakfast. This is Heidi.

Hi, we are driving up from Texas for our stay at your B&B later this month.

I am looking forward to meeting you and your family.

What will the weather be like?

Hmm, it could be 65 degrees and sunny ... or we could have 3 feet of snow.

Snow? But it will be the end of March, springtime.

I remember springtime. I grew up in Ohio, and yes, we did have spring there. Since moving here, I have realized Colorado has mostly two seasons: winter and summer.

Wow, it can snow that much in the spring?

Yes. Our state receives the majority of its snow during the months of March and April.

Whoa. How cold did you say it will be?

Anywhere from 10 degrees below zero to about 70 degrees.

Seriously?

Yes, and I'm talking about a 24-hour period.

Will my front-wheel drive car be good enough?

Most likely, but if not, I have a four-wheel drive truck. We'll make it work.

I guess I should bring warm clothes.

Yes, layers for different temperatures work great. There is a wood burner in the B&B that you will enjoy using. It is wonderful on those chilly nights and mornings. Oh ... along with your boots, I would throw in a pair of flip-flops.

Blueberry Scones

INGREDIENTS

⅓ cup butter

1¾ cup flour

3 Tablespoons sugar

2½ teaspoons baking powder

¼ teaspoon salt

1 egg, beaten

½–1 cup Half-and-Half cream

½ cup fresh blueberries (can use frozen/thawed)

Slivered almonds or walnut pieces

DIRECTIONS

- Mix dry ingredients.
- Slice small pieces of butter into dry ingredients and stir together.
- Stir in egg.
- Add fruit, mixing gently.
- Add enough Half-and-Half for dough to hold together.
- Pat out circle ½" thick on floured board.
- Cut into 8 wedges.
- Place scones on greased baking sheet.
- Brush with cream; sprinkle with sugar.
- Top with nut pieces.
- Bake @ 400F for 15-20 minutes until just beginning to brown.

International Guests

I had guests from all over the world. One family was from South Korea. The dad and son spoke English very fluently. I asked him what his work was, and he replied that he worked for the Office of Unification of South and North Korea. Wow, that's a tall order. He had my respect.

Note: The less you "mess" with the dough, the flakier the scones will be!
These are best eaten soon after they are baked.

My friend Gwen from Wales approved of this recipe – so I know it is a winner.

This recipe uses lots of bananas and it makes for a great, intense flavor. Any kind of gluten-free flour works, but I normally use rice or potato flour.

Banana Bread

Gluten Free

INGREDIENTS

2 cups gluten-free flour

1 teaspoon baking soda

¼ teaspoon salt

1 cup sugar

4 eggs

½ cup applesauce

⅓ cup oil

1 teaspoon vanilla

2 cups mashed ripe bananas

½ cup chopped walnuts

DIRECTIONS

- Preheat oven to 350F.
- Mix flour, soda, salt and sugar.
- Add eggs, applesauce, oil and vanilla.
- Stir in mashed bananas and nuts.
- Pour into 2 well-greased, sugared and lined (parchment paper) loaf pans.
- Bake 45-55 minutes or until toothpick in center comes out clean.
- These loaves freeze well.

HOPE

sees the

INVISIBLE

feels the

INTANGIBLE

and **achieves**

what is

IMPOSSIBLE

Mississippi Moments

I remember Bill and Wanda fondly … they arrived one Thanksgiving weekend during a cold, snowy and blustery day. The wood burner was going nonstop.

I loved talking with them over breakfast. They were from Mississippi, had wonderful accents and had led interesting lives. Wanda was a songwriter and had written a hit single that was used in a popular movie with John Travolta.

When they spoke of their town, I commented that it sounded like a place right out of a John Grisham novel. They said, "Well, it is. That's the area where he lived."

They told me a story of how every Little League baseball game turned into a request for the author to sign everyone's books.

He finally built a baseball diamond on his property and the games were held there with the condition that nobody asked him to autograph a book during a kids' ball game. Now I like John Grisham even more.

Wanda and I had a fun time Christmas shopping in the small town of Monument, and the sign she bought for me still hangs in my home today.

GOOD MEMORIES.

Almond Marzipan Bundt Cake

INGREDIENTS

1 cup margarine (2 sticks)

1½ cups sugar

1 teaspoon vanilla

1 teaspoon almond extract

3 eggs

1 cup sour cream

1 teaspoon baking powder

2¼ cups flour

INGREDIENTS (FILLING)

¾ cup almonds

½ teaspoon cinnamon

¼ cup sugar

8 ounces almond paste

DIRECTIONS

- Preheat oven to 350F.
- Cream butter and sugar.
- Add vanilla, almond extract, eggs, sour cream, baking powder and flour.
- Mix filling ingredients in blender.
- Grease and sugar a Bundt pan very thoroughly.
- Pour half of batter in pan and make groove all around batter halfway between sides and center.
- Place filling in groove.
- Pour remaining batter in pan and swirl a bit to mix filling.
- Place a few very thin slices of butter on top of batter.
- Bake 50-55 minutes.
- Before removing from pan, cool approximately 1 hour while loosening with knife around edges.
- Set pan on hot, wet towel in sink for 10 minutes and then invert on plate. It should come out clean.

Texas Gentlemen

I have had so many wonderful guests visit the B&B, and many of them were from Texas. They loved our scenic state, weather and green grass! It was always fun to see the kids enjoying the yard and hear the adults comment on how cool it was in the shade. A nice reprieve from a hot, southern summer.

I was always amazed at how gracious and appreciative guests were. One party consisted of three adult brothers whose wives had stayed home while the men drove to Colorado to share time together with an elderly aunt and cousins in the area. I loved their accents. Before heading out one morning to visit their extended family, they called out a good-bye from downstairs.

Then one of them said, "Heidi (pronounced Haaaady), is there anything you need from the grocery store? We'll be making a stop." I laughed and said, "Sure, I'll give you my list." Joking, of course, but I did thank them for their generosity. They probably would have prepared the breakfast, as well, if I had asked them to.

Time and time again I had guests walk upstairs in the morning, examine the coffee/tea bar and gaze at the breakfast buffet spread out on the counter. They would then say, "Wow, this is an amazing breakfast! What a nice surprise!"

I was always amazed that guests didn't expect this kind of breakfast. It was certainly wonderful to hear the appreciation. What a rewarding experience.

Almond paste is found in the baking aisle by the pie fillings. It is usually sold in a roll. If you cannot find it, the almond filling which is sold in a can will do.

Marzipan is a German confection that is a combination of almond paste, powdered sugar and egg whites. It can be dyed with food coloring and shaped to resemble fruits, vegetables or anything you wish.

My mom was a perfectionist with this, making bananas, strawberries, oranges, lemons and pears. This was a yearly Christmas treat for our family. She did a great job making them, and we did a wonderful job of eating them.

Cherry Nut Coffee Cake

INGREDIENTS

1 cup sugar

2 cups flour

1 teaspoon baking powder

1 teaspoon baking soda

¼ teaspoon salt

½ cup butter

2 eggs

1 cup sour cream

INGREDIENTS (TOPPING)

⅓ cup sugar

½ cup chopped nuts

16 oz. maraschino cherries (drained and chopped)

1½ teaspoons cinnamon

DIRECTIONS

- Grease and flour tube pan well.
- Mix sugar, flour, baking powder, baking soda, salt, butter and eggs.
- Fold in sour cream.
- Pour all of batter into pan.
- Mix topping ingredients and sprinkle over top.
- Swirl topping into batter.
- Bake @ 375F for 30 minutes.
- Cool approximately an hour, then loosen cake from pan by gently inserting table knife and running it around outside of cake edge.
- Remove cake from pan and continue to cool on rack.
- Place on plate or cake platter and cover well.

This cake is tasty and moist but be careful not to overbake or it will dry out.

I am not a fan of buying maraschino cherries, but they do taste great in this recipe. It is colorful and would be nice during the Christmas holidays.

You might mix green and red cherries to add extra festiveness.

117

Hugging Trees

These Culturally Modified Trees are in nearby Fox Run Park.
Snow really brings out the characteristics and uniqueness of each tree.

Portal Tree

Snow and Santa Claus Visits

I remember this one Texan family well – the parents and two young boys aged four and six. They were so excited for their Colorado visit over Christmas and called me ahead of time to ask if there would be snow.

I said, "I hope so!" Anyone living in the Colorado Springs area knows we could have a blizzard, lots of snow, no snow or 65 degrees on Christmas.

Thank goodness the weather cooperated and while they were here the beautiful white fluff arrived, blanketing the ground with several inches. The boys went sledding and were so excited for Christmas.

One evening the doorbell rang and one of my best friends, Laurie, was standing there with two of her guests for the holidays ... one I recognized as her sister but the other looked suspiciously like Santa Claus.

We called the boys up from the B&B and their eyes grew huge when they popped up the stairs and saw Santa Claus in the rocker by the Christmas tree.

What a perfect evening and fun memory for all of us. Santa has an uncanny knack for perfect timing.

Lemon Pudding Cake

INGREDIENTS

1½ cups sugar

½ cup flour

3 Tablespoons butter, melted

1½ cups milk

3 eggs, separated

1 lemon (grate rind and squeeze
   lemon for juice)

DIRECTIONS

- Beat egg whites on high speed until stiff, then set aside.
- Mix flour, sugar and melted butter.
- Add milk, egg yolks, lemon juice and grated rind.
- Mix well and then gently fold in egg whites.
- Pour into greased 9" x 9" pan.
- Bake @ 350F for 50 minutes.
- Sprinkle with powdered sugar before serving, or top with whipped cream and a few blueberries or raspberries.
- Refrigerate any leftovers.

This treat is best after allowing to refrigerate for at least 3-4 hours and can definitely stay in overnight.

Camping Anyone?

This can be for brunch or dessert. It always reminds me of summer with its rich, lemony flavor.

One summer I had a couple rent a camping space on my property. This was a first-time experience for all of us. They had sold their home, bought a trailer and had to live somewhere while their new home was being built.

It was one of those situations where their request came across my field of vision, I contacted them, and they showed up the next day with camper in tow!

They were wonderful people, and it was really nice to look out towards the barn and see them enjoying the space under the trees with their two little dogs. When I worked on the property or in the garden, we would visit, and they would offer help and advice. There was definitely an emptiness after they had gone.

Light – flavorful – touch of lemon for a light breakfast or a midday treat.

Lemon Poppy Muffins

INGREDIENTS

¼ pound (1 stick) butter or margarine

⅔ cup sugar

2 eggs

1 cup vanilla yogurt or sour cream
(can also use flavored yogurt)

2 cups flour

1 teaspoon baking soda

1 Tablespoon lemon zest (grated
lemon rind)

3 Tablespoons poppy seeds

GLAZE

Fresh lemon juice (enough for pouring consistency)

2 Tablespoons sugar

DIRECTIONS

- Cream butter/margarine and sugar.
- Add eggs, beating well after each addition.
- Mix flour and baking soda.
- Alternate folding in flour/soda mixture and yo-gurt, beginning and ending with flour/soda.
- Fold in lemon zest and poppy seeds with last of flour.
- Fill approximately 15-16 muffin tins (paper lined) about three quarters full.
- Bake for 15-20 minutes @ 350F.
- Stir sugar with small amount of lemon juice and brush over warm muffins.

What Time Is It Anyways?

Sometimes I really was in a rush getting everything cleaned and ready for the next guests to arrive. Thanks to the help of my great friend Cheri (who could vacuum carpet and oil baseboards at the drop of a hat), the timeline was usually met!

These muffins have a short prep and baking time, so they were a great recipe for afternoons. It is wonderfully inviting to have that freshly-baked aroma when folks walk through the front door.

When check-in time begins at 3:00pm, many guests are going to arrive before 3:00pm, like 2:45pm – you get the idea. Of course, whenever any of us travel we tend to stay in our home time zone for a while.

I was washing my hair when I heard the doorbell ring. I quickly wrapped my head in a towel and peeked out the front window. Yep, there were my guests at 1:45pm. (They were from Missouri.)

Feeling funny opening the door with a towel on my head, I called out the window, "I'll be there in just a minute." This is, of course, a less-than-ideal method of greeting guests.

A couple of minutes later I opened the door and let them in. They apologized and said, "Sorry we were a few minutes early."

Well, they used the Central time zone so that explained the confusion. I welcomed them in and laugh about it now.

It definitely trained me to always be ready way ahead of time as I didn't want to be in that situation again.

I was brought up not to waste, and to this day I try really hard to stick to that. I miss raising chickens because they were so good at leftovers!

Squash / Zucchini Bread

Moist ... delicious ... and a great way to put all those garden zucchinis to use.

INGREDIENTS

3 cups sugar

3½ cups flour

1 teaspoon baking powder

2 teaspoons baking soda

2 teaspoons salt

2 teaspoons ground cloves

2 teaspoons cinnamon

4 eggs

½ cup oil

3 cups grated zucchini/squash

1 cup walnuts, chopped (optional)

DIRECTIONS

- In large bowl, stir together sugar, flour, baking powder, baking soda, salt, cloves and cinnamon.
- Add eggs, oil and grated zucchini.
- Stir well by hand until all ingredients are combined.
- Stir in walnuts.
- Place in 2 greased, floured and lined loaf pans.
- Bake @ 325F for approximately 60 minutes or until inserted toothpick comes out clean.
- Check near end of bake time and loosely lay foil over top if browning too quickly.
- Cool in pans before removing.

With the B&B I buy quality ingredients, but not in excess. If you are making scones, use "cream not milk" kind of mindset. In fact, if you have cream on hand, you can substitute it for milk in most recipes in this book.

Bread Pudding

INGREDIENTS

8 Kaiser rolls

1 quart whipping cream

6 eggs

1 cup sugar

⅓ cup golden raisins

3 Tablespoons butter

DIRECTIONS

- Cut rolls into large crouton-size cubes and place in large bowl.
- Add cream and let soften 10-15 minutes, stirring with spatula frequently.
- In large mixing bowl, beat eggs until frothy – beat in sugar.
- Add raisins and pour mixture over bread. Fold in gently but thoroughly.
- Melt butter in 8" x 12" dish, add bread mixture and spread evenly.
- Bake @ 350F for 50 minutes – cool.
- Top with vanilla sauce (next page).

This is my mom's recipe – and a crowd favorite. Make the vanilla sauce (following page) first and refrigerate before making bread pudding.

Vanilla Sauce for Bread Pudding

Do you really need to make this vanilla sauce for the bread pudding? YES!

INGREDIENTS

5 egg yolks

½ cup sugar

1 Tablespoon corn starch

2½ cups Half-and-Half cream

½ vanilla bean

1 teaspoon vanilla

DIRECTIONS

- Beat egg yolks and sugar until thick and lemon-colored.
- In a saucepan, dissolve the cornstarch in ½ cup cream.
- Add the remaining cream and vanilla bean.
- Bring to a boil, stirring constantly.
- Gradually pour hot mixture into egg/sugar mix and blend well.
- Return to heat, stirring constantly until mixture thickens.
- Cool while stirring frequently. Pour into pitcher and refrigerate.
- Stir before serving. If too thick, add some more cream.
- Serve over warm bread pudding.

Who's Cooking?

During the winter when the B&B season was slower, I would often host long-term renters. This worked great for Marlene, Gregg and their dog Roxie.

 Instead of cooking meals I would share my kitchen. Marlene was quite a cook and would usually text me that a "plate" was waiting for me on the counter ... so this setup was quite a bonus for me as well.

I served this Bread Pudding one Easter when they were there, along with some of my family, and we fed quite a large table of guests with it ... and still had leftovers. Another crowd pleaser.

Very tasty and great when eaten warm right out of the oven. Serve with butter/whipped cream and jam.

Cranberry Orange Scones

INGREDIENTS

2 cups flour

10 teaspoons sugar, divided

1 tablespoon grated orange peel (or lemon)

2 teaspoons baking powder

¼ teaspoon baking soda

½ teaspoon salt

⅓ cup cold butter

1 cup dried cranberries

¼ cup Half-and-Half cream

¼ cup orange juice

1 large egg

1 Tablespoon milk

DIRECTIONS

- Combine flour, 7 teaspoons sugar, orange peel, baking powder, salt and soda.
- Cut in butter – set aside.
- Combine cranberries, orange juice, cream and egg. Add to flour mixture and stir briefly until soft dough forms. Do not over-stir.
- On floured board, gently knead 6-10 times (less is better for flakiness).
- Pat into 8-inch circle and cut into 10 wedges.
- Place on greased baking sheet and brush scones with milk – sprinkle with sugar.
- Bake @ 400F for 15 minutes.

Cream's the Answer

I tried these out on my friend Gwen, from Wales ... the ultimate test.

She definitely approved and asked if I used cream. I said "Yes," and she replied "Good, always use cream with scones. Always. That is the secret." Seems I've heard her say that before.

Wildflowers in the back forest.

The Chapter Ends

In some ways, life is like a book – when one chapter ends, a new one begins. They build on each other, intertwine and overlap.

The home that housed Fox Run Bed & Breakfast had several chapters, initially being built as a custom home, then used as a corporate home and in 1995 our family moved in after being drawn to the property by its lush and woodsy setting on the edge of the Black Forest.

Animals filled the barn and pasture. Kids, friends and fellow 4-H'ers spent endless hours caring for the animals, playing with springtime baby goats and collecting eggs from the chicken coop. At times it resembled a petting zoo. The kids described it as the best place to spend their childhood. The neighbors were like family.

As the page turned to another chapter, young children grew up, moved on to make their own lives and the roomy raised-ranch home longed for others to enjoy it and its tranquil setting. It was meant to be shared. Fox Run B&B was born with guests coming from around the world to see the sights of Colorado Springs and surrounding areas during the days, and at night they would retreat to the calm setting tucked away in the forest.

These years were spent hosting wonderful people – some came as families, others met up with friends, still others arrived to attend reunions, and some held their weddings on the large green lawn surrounded by quiet woods. Memorable times, happy people, long conversations around the breakfast table and lively times with lots of laughter. People from all walks of life flowed in and out of those doors, and I was lucky enough to get acquainted with them all. Many returned time and time again.

In 2019 the writing of another chapter was in the works. The bed and breakfast experience had been so rewarding and enriching. However, I wished to free up some time to visit my grown kids and their families around the country, to work on projects such as this book and dedicate more energy to our non-profit NASTaP (Native American Sacred Trees and Places). The decision to move on was bittersweet.

The spark of this book began with my guests suggesting I publish my recipes that they enjoyed. Close friends encouraged me, and it became a reality. The people, stories and recipes are woven together in this book. May you enjoy the anecdotes and have people to share the recipes with in making memories of your own.

I am further inspired to write about and share another passion of mine, honoring sacred places on our earth. My dream is to help bring awareness and appreciation of some very special sites, trees and the energy they encompass. They merit preservation, as does our earth and all it has to offer. By caring for our planet, we can all benefit and live more in harmony with it. Stay tuned.

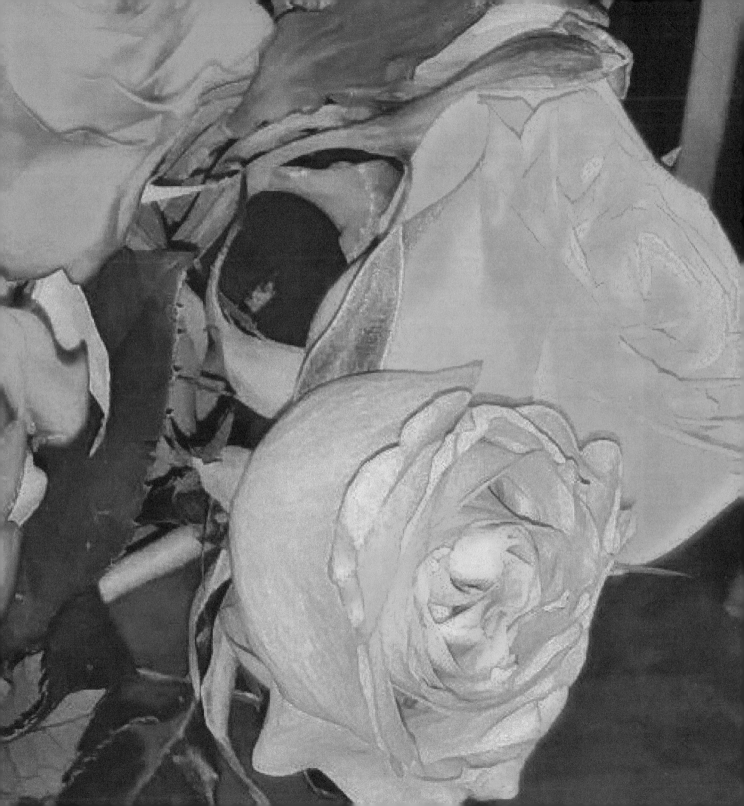

Acknowledgements

This book would not have been possible without running the B&B, so not only do I wish to acknowledge those who encouraged me with the book-writing process, but I also owe a huge thanks to those who were so supportive of Fox Run Bed and Breakfast.

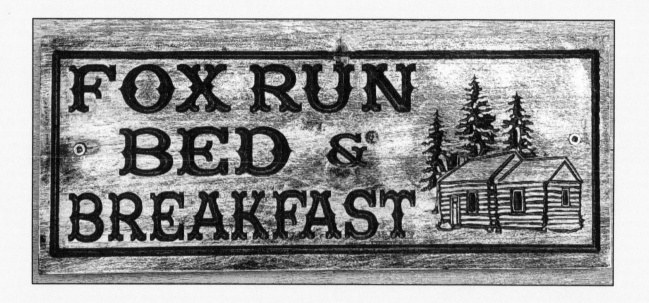

Thank You

JOHN: Your initial encouragement helped make my decision to write this book. I appreciate all your advice and support during the process, the writing workshops you held and the example you set of becoming an author, including "tighten" and "brighten". Also, your enthusiasm and promotion of the B&B was much appreciated and made for some great breakfast conversations with guests from all walks of life.

ROB: Your enormous gift of time in formatting this book is unmatched. I appreciate your friendship, talents, sharp mind, honesty and humor while working on this project and always. Your formatting work and amazing ability to work through obstacles, along with your thorough knowledge of creating a book from start to finish made this book happen. What a HUGE undertaking; THANK YOU.

MIKE: I owe you many thanks in creating the cover design and back. You captured the essence of the B&B perfectly. I hope to meet in person one day.

TYLER: Thank you for your work with Mike in creating the cover design, your advice on the title and book specifics, your proofreading, editing and index help, and sound advice on all aspects of the book. How lucky for me that this is your day job too, and that you are so good at it.

HOLLY: Thank you for your encouragement during the writing process. I appreciate your proofreading as well, just to make sure there are no incriminating "growing up" stories I might have snuck in. The gift of the Fox Run Bed and Breakfast sign early on at the start of the business was a treasure, and I display it proudly.

ALEX: Even though you live afar, the times you were home were filled with hands-on work ... from perfectly-cut crown molding to installation with the proper tools and the construction of the most awesome firepit for the B&B guests to enjoy. Thanks also for your proofreading and help in sampling any recipe I made when you were home.

CODY: I appreciate your help and input with the book and photos, and for proofreading the entire file. I remember the fun you had building the outdoor firepit with Alex, and it was enjoyed by many of the B&B guests. I know the visitors appreciated your tiptoeing around when you did visit.

JENNA, MEGAN AND LEAH: Thank you all for your support and interest in the B&B and this book, for planning your visits around guest reservations and for keeping the boys in line when you were able to visit.

ALL MY KIDS: Thank you for your support and understanding that your former rooms were transformed in your absence and that you needed a reservation to come home.

CHERI: You were a constant encouragement and always willing to help at the drop of a hat. Thank you for your friendship, food sampling, exercise partnership, woodwork oil-soaping skills and willingness to help with whatever was needed at the time.

LAURIE: Thank you for being that friend who knows me so well. Your enthusiasm in making the "tourist notebooks" and journal were so appreciated. Your sound advice, recipes and boosting my confidence was so helpful. Your raking skills after a gutter cleaning are unmatched, and you knew I needed help that day! I appreciate your helpful review and great suggestions.

and DAVE: I so appreciated your recipe contributions, food quality control, leftover management and -visual assistance. So many wires. Thanks for being there whenever I needed anything.

BRIGITTE, MAURICE, EMMA and DICKENS: You were wonderful guests and good hiking buddies with a great sense of humor. You then moved here and became close friends. I am grateful for you all.

BARB, WARREN and VANESSA: I appreciate your thoughtful B&B gift contributions (think chalkboards, no matter how small), website scrutiny, undying encouragement and advice on using butter to brown those potatoes. I appreciate your friendship and your insistent invitations for me to come have a drink, dinner and relax. I especially appreciate your review and helpful suggestions (my book now has an ending!).

GWEN: Thank you for your friendship that I value greatly, wonderful phone conversations and continuous encouragement for all my endeavors. Even though you don't live near, your support is present and means a lot. We always have a lot to talk and laugh about.

RUTA: I love and appreciate your spirit and enthusiasm. You are uplifting to be around. Thank you for adopting me so I could have two moms.

CHRIS: Thank you for your brains and time in creating the website I would not have had otherwise. Really.

BLANDINE: Thank you for understanding my time needed to complete my book and your help in promoting it. I'm glad we met and got to know each other and appreciate the opportunity to have worked at The French Kitchen. Who knows, one day I may surprise you and teach a cooking class.

SEBASTIAN: I really appreciate your constant encouragement by asking, "Is your book done yet?" Seriously, I enjoyed seeing a master bakery chef at work.

ANNE: Thank you for your enthusiasm and sparking the idea of virtual presentations for my recipes. You have a great spark about you.

BARB H. and CAROL: Thank you for your help with physical labor, whether fence-building or vacuuming, and for your willingness to taste and scrutinize food dishes.

KATHLEEN, TRIVIAN, KAREN, LISA and TISH: I treasure our laughter, get-togethers, bonding even when we are apart, and your wonderful gifts that added a special touch.

PAM, LYNDA and KIM: You are my roots, supporting me from afar and knowing me to the core. I feel your presence always.

JUDY and JANIE: I appreciate your encouragement and support through the years.

NEIGHBORS: I was surrounded by all of you during my B&B business. Thank you for your snow-plowing, pasture mowing and never complaining about noise or a field of parked cars.

ALL MY GUESTS: You all made this entire endeavor so worthwhile and rewarding. The B&B would not have been without you all. Thank you.

JESSE: You are the best dog ever and made all the canine guests feel at home. Your willingness to sample every single food morsel has not gone unnoticed.

Index

oranges, 2, 34, 115
palachinke, 41
paprika, 14, 48
parsley, 59
peaches, 4, 76
peanut butter, 30
peanuts, 24
pears, 24, 115
pecans, 24, 76, 85, 93
peel, lemon, 28, 102, 133
peel, orange, 2, 133
pepper, 13, 14, 48, 51, 56,
  60, 69, 75, 79, 80
peppermints, 24
peppers, 13, 17, 48, 59, 69
pie crust, 56, 60, 75
pineapple, 24
potato, 13, 17, 140
pudding, 130
pumpkin, 89, 93
raisins, 128
ramekin, 4
raspberries, 4, 76, 120
rice, 80, 108

rolls, 128
rosemary, 102, 103
salmon, 78, 79
salsa, 25, 49
salt, coarse, 30, 102
sausage, 42, 56, 69
schnapps, 10
scones, 106, 107, 127, 133,
  134
sea salt, 102
seasoned salt, 55
shallots, 14
sour cream, 2, 9, 17, 43,
  49, 59, 62, 95, 113, 116,
  123
soy, 80
spinach, 60, 61, 69
sprinkles, 27
squash, 126
strawberries, 2, 4, 15, 22,
  24, 26, 29, 34, 41, 43,
  76, 115
swiss cheese, 55, 59, 60,
  79

syrup, 41, 43, 66, 76
Tabasco, 75
tapioca, 80
tarragon, 14
tea, 35, 84, 98, 114
Thanksgiving, 111
tomato, 13, 14, 48, 59, 60,
  61, 69, 80
tortillas, 48, 68
turkey, 48, 50, 51, 69, 70
vanilla, 18, 19, 30, 43, 76,
  87, 95, 100, 109, 113, 130
vanilla bean, 130
walnuts, 24, 76, 85, 93,
  100, 106, 109, 126
water, flavored, 34, 35
whipping cream, 75, 94,
  128
white coating, 22, 24, 27
yogurt, 2, 4, 9, 11, 15, 76,
  123
yogurt bar, 11, 15, 42
zest, lemon, 102, 123
zucchini, 126